D0342297

ALSO BY LYNNE HYBELS
AND BILL HYBELS

*Rediscovering Church: The Story and Vision of
Willow Creek Community Church*

Fit to Be Tied: Making Marriage Last a Lifetime

nice girls
don't change
the world

nice girls don't change the world

lynne hybels

ZONDERVAN™

GRAND RAPIDS, MICHIGAN 49530 USA

WILLOW
Willow Creek Resources

ZONDERVAN.COM/
AUTHOR**TRACKER**

We want to hear from you. Please send
your comments about this book to us in care
of zreview@zondervan.com. Thank you.

ZONDERVAN.COM/
AUTHOR**TRACKER**

ZONDERVAN™

Nice Girls Don't Change the World
Copyright © 2005 by Lynne Hybels

Requests for information should be addressed to:

Willow Creek Association
P.O. Box 3188, Barrington, Illinois 60011-3188

or

Zondervan, *Grand Rapids, Michigan 49530*

ISBN-10: 0-310-27231-9
ISBN-13: 978-0-310-27231-1

This edition printed on acid-free paper.

Photo credits are located on page 96.

Book design by Cheryl Blum

Printed in the United States of America

06 07 08 09 10 11 • 12 11 10 9 8 7 6 5 4 3 2

For my mother, Leah Keyser Barry,
and my daughter, Shauna Hybels Niequist

nice girls
don't change
the world

I WANT TO TELL YOU about someone I used to know very well.

She was a nice girl: obedient, polite, socially acceptable. A bit too reticent, some might say, but so very pleasing, nonetheless. A really nice girl.

Oh yes, her gaze seemed empty at times and her words sometimes rang, well, not false really, but perhaps a bit flat.

Okay, I sometimes had the feeling she was just going through the motions of life, but they were such nice motions. Everybody liked her.

She had an uncanny ability to keep almost everybody happy almost all the time, though she didn't truly seem to be very happy herself. But I could be wrong; she was always smiling. I don't know that I ever heard her laugh—and no one ever accused her of being wildly in love with life—but she had such a nice smile.

She was a very caring person, though in a passive sort of way. She was not the type to turn the world upside down.

Still, she was a very nice girl.

What I mean to say, as you might have guessed, is that *I* was a very nice girl.

A nice girl. There's nothing wrong with being a nice girl, especially when you consider the alternatives:

A naughty girl?

A mean girl?

A bad girl?

Who wants to be like that? I didn't.

I *really* didn't.

What I wanted was to be a godly girl. From the time I became a Christian at age seven, I wanted to please God, and I took that desire very seriously.

a nice girl

I grew up in the 1950s and '60s in a small Michigan town, where I attended a church that was a fine church in many ways. But the preaching during my most impressionable years was pretty much hellfire and brimstone. I heard a lot about sin and punishment, guilt and shame.

....

I was a very sensitive little girl. Based on what I'd heard about God, I concluded that the only way to earn the favor of this hard-hearted demanding deity was to work very hard, be very good, and walk a very straight and narrow path.

So I did. At age ten I traded my ballet slippers for a flute because I'd been taught that dancing was a sin—but making music was an acceptable form of worship. From that time on, I tried very hard to make what I thought were God-honoring decisions about life. If there were rules to follow, I followed them. If there were pleasures to give up, I gave them up. If there was work to do, I did it. I was determined to earn God's love.

I was also convinced that part of earning God's love was earning everybody else's love too—pleasing everybody, keeping everybody happy, being very nice.

Every morning I got out of bed and prayed: *Dear God, what am I supposed to do today? Just tell me and I'll do it. Anything.* I seldom got a clear answer, which was very frustrating because I knew how important it was to get it right. How could I keep myself under the umbrella of God's favor if I didn't get everything right?

So I kept trying.

For years I tried: I prayed, read my Bible, and worked harder and harder in the hope that one day I would experience what this whole Christian thing was supposed to be about. I hoped that one day I would feel God's love, know it deep inside, and at last be able to rest in it.

But you can only work hard and seek love for so long. Eventually you just run out of energy. And I did.

At that point I had been a pastor's wife for seventeen years. At twenty-two, I was delighted to marry a man who felt called to the ministry— I felt called too. I never viewed starting a church as something I was obligated to do because of who I was married to; I *wanted* to do it. But after seventeen years I was so exhausted I didn't want to get out of bed. In fact, to state it plainly, I didn't want to go on living. Later I came to understand that I was not just tired—I was seriously depressed.

Most people didn't know the state I was in. I was still pretty good at going through the nice girl motions, but things were definitely not nice on the inside. Fighting the all-too-common myth that only certifiably crazy people seek professional help, I decided to see a Christian counselor.

In counseling I heard for the first time that there is an alternative to being a "nice girl," and it has nothing to do with being naughty, or mean, or bad.

a good woman

The opposite of a nice girl, I learned, is a

"good woman." Being

a good woman means

trading the safe,

passive, people-pleasing

behavior of niceness for

the dynamic power of true goodness.

It means moving from the weakness

and immaturity of girlhood toward the

strength and maturity of womanhood.

....

Whereas a girl of any age lives out the script she learned as a child—a script too often grounded in powerlessness—a woman acknowledges and accepts her power to change, and grow, and be a force for good in the world.

Whereas a nice girl tends to live according to the will of others, a good woman has only one goal: to discern and live out the will of God.

A good woman knows that her ultimate calling in life is to be part of God's plan for redeeming all things in this sin-touched world.

A good woman knows she cannot be all things to all people, and she may, in fact, displease those who think she should just be nice. She is not strident or petty or demanding, but she does live according to conviction. She knows that the Jesus she follows was a revolutionary who never tried to keep everyone happy.

That picture of a good woman made me want to be one. It made me want to grow up and trade the innocuous acceptability of niceness for the world-changing power and passion of true goodness.

I was thirty-nine years old when I walked into my counselor's office and said, "I've been working so hard to keep everybody else happy, but I'm so miserable I want to die." I spent the decade of my forties digging out of that hole. Now, nearly midway through my fifties, I've discovered that growing up is an ongoing process—I have not yet arrived. Still, I have learned some things on the journey to becoming a good woman.

....

*A good woman's life
is grounded in the love of God.*

I've learned that a good woman's life is grounded in the love of God. In my thirties, I would have told you that my life was grounded in God's love because that's what my adult mind believed. My rational, all-grown-up theology assured me God did, in fact, love me.

In reality, however, I was not living out what my adult mind believed, but what my childhood mind believed. This was a theology grounded not in the assurance of God's love, but in my own desperate striving to earn that love.

....

After nearly thirty-five years of that kind of striving, I was exhausted—physically, emotionally, and spiritually.

The first thing my counselor told me—quite emphatically, I might add—was to get off the treadmill and rest. This should have been welcome news, but it wasn't. The God of my childhood would not let me rest. This God demanded action, service, work, striving. Rest was simply out of the question. Yet I knew I needed to rest, and I knew I needed to radically change my life. I could not face the future if it was just going to be a repeat of the past. I couldn't do it.

When I considered embracing the rest I so desperately needed, I knew it would require a momentous and scary decision: I could only rest if I got rid of my childhood God.

On a hot summer day in 1991, I stretched out on my back on the deck of a little sailboat, looked up into the clouds, and addressed the God of my childhood.

"I can't do it anymore," I said. "I can't keep striving for your love. Maybe there is a God somewhere who doesn't drain the life out of people, but I don't know who that God is. You're the only God I know, and I can't carry the burden of *you* anymore."

I had never called God a burden. I knew the right words to say about God: *God is my strength, my refuge, my helper in time of need. God is my gracious father, my tender mother, the lover of my soul.* But despite these benevolent phrases that I knew so well, what God really felt like was a horrible weight dragging me down.

So I turned my back on the God of my childhood. I was not trying to be rebellious; if there's anything I never wanted to be it was rebellious. But I could no longer carry the burden of such a harsh and demanding deity.

As the ultimate nice girl and striver after divine favor, it was no small thing to turn my back on God. I didn't broadcast this decision. I was still a pastor's wife. I didn't want to confuse people or shake anyone else's faith, but I was done with a God who daily sucked the life out of me—and I was too tired to search for a replacement.

In retrospect, I see it more like this: the true God, in grace, set me free. Even in my desperation, I don't believe I would have had the courage to walk away from my childhood God unless the Spirit of a different God had

. . . .

whispered in my ear: *I understand. I know your soul needs to be purged and healed from the wound of the false God. So, do it. Turn your back. Walk away. It'll be okay.*

So I dropped the burden of my childhood God and I rested. There were still tasks and duties I simply had to muster the energy to attend to. But whenever possible, I did the only thing I truly had energy for: I sat in an easy chair and looked out the window.

At first I felt horribly guilty about these quiet unproductive moments. I tried to fight the exhaustion. I'd think, "Okay, today I'll get busy again. I'll prove my worth again. I'll chase God's love again." But I couldn't do it. I didn't have the energy. So, once again, in the free

moments of my days, I took up my post by the window.

I sat there and watched the summer leaves take on the colors of autumn, and the fall rain turn to snow. I watched birds perched in a crabapple tree, and squirrels playing tag in my yard. I still felt guilty and utterly useless, but I couldn't deny that something deep was beginning to stir in me as I yielded to the beauties of nature.

As fall turned to winter, I built fires in the fireplace; listened to music; sipped fragrant, steaming teas; and lingered over the pages of art books. Alone in my bedroom, with the drapes drawn, sometimes I even danced. I felt like a little girl again—not a nice girl seeking to

please, but a playful child free to enjoy the simple pleasures of life—and I became increasingly convinced that that's how I needed to be.

An amazing thing happened. My body began to recuperate but, even more, my soul came to life, and as it did I began to long for a God again. Not the God of my childhood, certainly. But some God. Alone at night in bed, when Bill was out of town and the kids were asleep, I sometimes had the sense that there was a Presence there, that I was not alone in the universe, that there was something, someone, to whom my soul was drawn.

I decided to open my heart just a crack to this mysterious Presence, knowing that if I heard even one syllable of the demanding rhetoric of my childhood God, I could immediately slam shut the door to my heart—and I was fully prepared to do that.

But I decided to take a little risk.

Into the void, I whispered two simple words. "It's me."

What I heard—or sensed—in response was a whisper as soft as my own.

I love you, the whisperer said. *Right here. Right now. I love you so much that I want you to rest. I want you to sit and receive the refreshment of my creation. I want you to listen to music. I want you to dance in the quietness of your bedroom. I want you to be like a child, secure and free in the presence of an adoring parent.*

I want you to know that all those years when you were working so hard to try to please me, I was trying to tell you to slow down. I saw you killing yourself from the inside out and I tried to stop you. But the many false voices in your head drowned out the single true voice in your heart.

. . . .

I wasn't the one cracking the whip, the one telling you to work harder, the one who made you feel guilty when you relaxed. I was the one who saw you, who knew you, who believed in you, who longed to restore your energy. I was the one trying to fluff up the pillow, tuck the blanket around your shoulders, and tell you it was time to rest. I was the one trying to love you.

I have described this brief encounter with that loving Presence many times, and yet every time I type it onto another page, I weep again.

I think when I am on my deathbed, I will recall that moment as the pivotal moment of my life. To be truly embraced by the love of God changes everything.

Knowing oneself loved by God is not a matter of knowing about God's love. It's not a matter of saying the right words or even claiming the right beliefs. It's about something that happens on a level deeper than words and ideas and knowledge and thoughts. It's something that gets inside one's soul and never leaves.

I don't know why God graced me with such an extraordinary experience. Maybe it's because the absolute failure of my own wisdom and energy left an internal emptiness into which the true God could enter and speak. If that's true, then I consider my depression, my exhaustion, my complete inability to get on with life, as the best thing that could have happened to me.

Whereas in the past my Christianity was focused on work and effort and striving, I can honestly say that the center from which my spiritual life flows today is the time I set aside daily to be silent in the presence of God, emptying my mind as best I can of words and thoughts, and simply inviting God to fill that open space. Every time I do this I feel as if I fall into a well of love—a love that centers me, calms me, and heals me on deeper levels than my conscious mind understands.

Paradoxically, it is out of this quiet resting that I hear God's call to compassionate action in the world, but it is a very gentle thing. In it is none of the trauma and anxiety I experienced in the past. This is a radically different way to do ministry. It's ministry that flows out of fullness and joy and gratitude for life—what Frederick Buechner describes as that point where "your deep gladness and the world's deep hunger meet." It's the kind of ministry—the kind of life—I believe God calls all of us to, but it has to be grounded in a true, daily experience of God's love.

Perhaps you already know and experience God's love this way. But maybe, like me, you've clung to a toxic notion of God leftover from your childhood. Or it could be you have just been so caught up in the busyness of life that you haven't taken the time to let God love you.

My hope is that as you read this book you will experience a moment of rest and release, that you will let your shoulders drop, take a deep breath, and relax. We want to give to others, but we must first receive. I pray that you will hear the gentle whisper of God's love for you, even now, so that your life can be grounded in that love.

A good woman knows
her unique life matters to God.

Another thing I've learned about a good woman is that she understands she is not just loved in some generic way, as an anonymous human being, but she is loved as an individual, a one-of-a-kind creation. She knows that her personality, her gifts, her passions, her dreams —her unique life—matters to God.

If you had asked me in my twenties and thirties if that was true, I would have said, "Of course." But I didn't live like it was true. Actually, I lived as if everybody else's "unique life" mattered, but mine didn't.

Many women tend to pay more attention to other people's lives than to their own. But nice girls elevate that skill to an art form.

Shortly after I started counseling, my counselor asked why I looked at the world through Bill's eyes. "I don't," I said, and then I spent the next year proving that I did.

For months I could not answer the counselor's questions without voicing Bill's perceptions, Bill's values, Bill's insights and opinions. It would have been comic if it weren't so sad. I knew far more about Bill than I knew about myself. I knew his gifts and temperament, his strengths and weaknesses, his needs and desires, his passions and calling, his dreams, his recreational interests, his long-range goals, his

preferred spiritual disciplines. But I knew none of these things about myself.

There is a vast collection of reasons why that was true, but topping the list was this: Bill's ministry was so demanding and so fruitful—and so obviously valuable—that I gradually slid into believing my quieter, less visible life could not possibly matter as much as his. What was important was to keep Bill going, make *his* life manageable, facilitate *his* ministry.

Bill didn't ask for that from me, but it's what I perceived as right. I grew up in an era and a tradition in which I was taught—or at least I picked up—that the highest calling of a woman (if married) was to "enhance" her husband's life, so he could go out into the world and make his mark. If a woman had children she should do the same for them. Though my own mother never once suggested I follow these mandates, I took them to heart.

I would never have said that my life didn't matter, but I ended up living as if it didn't.

When Bill and I started a church, I was very young and didn't yet know what I was good at. I had never even heard of spiritual gifts, those divinely empowered abilities that enable us to minister effectively. I just knew I wanted to serve God and other people in any way I could.

In the early years of the church, I was in the music ministry, playing the flute in our church orchestra, which I loved. I also enjoyed

writing, so I wrote articles for church publications. I was a young mom, so I started a ministry for other young moms.

But as the church grew and Bill got busier, I picked up virtually all of the time-consuming practicalities of keeping a home and family going, as well as a growing list of duties related to being a pastor's wife, leaving less and less time for anything else. Over the years my life became increasingly focused on household chores, secretarial tasks, administrative details, and entertaining.

There is nothing wrong with any of these activities, but for reasons I could not understand, I found myself hating life. I really didn't know why. I figured I must be a really selfish, demanding person who wasn't willing to do what God asked me to do. I tried to change my attitude, but I grew increasingly miserable. The unhappier I became, the guiltier I felt, and the more I confessed my sin. I became convinced I was a really bad Christian, and I believed that for years.

It wasn't until my counselor helped me look more honestly at my natural abilities and spiritual gifts that I realized what was really wrong. I am not by nature a task-oriented person; I am not good at handling details or complexity; and I have not one shred of such gifts as administration, helps, or hospitality. It was a stunning discovery to realize I had spent years shaping my life around gifts I did not have. Not only that, I had completely neglected the gifts I did have.

My true gifts are encouragement, mercy, and discernment. I would much rather deal with people than tasks. I find human beings endlessly fascinating, whereas tasks and details always frustrate me. I also love dealing with words and ideas. I felt called to write, but writing requires time and solitude, neither of which I had.

Obviously, at that point I should have made changes in my life, but I didn't. Oh, I made half-hearted stabs at it: I talked to Bill and the kids about creating a more equitable way of handling responsibilities at home so I could carve out time to devote elsewhere. I repeatedly considered getting administrative help to handle the church-related details that consumed so much of my energy. But I didn't do it.

It wasn't that I wanted a full-time career or ministry outside the home. Though I genuinely celebrate women who are free to make that choice, it was not my aspiration, nor do I believe it would have been realistic for our family. But I could not shake the longing—which I now see as a clear manifestation of God's calling on my life—to use my true gifts consistently in some way.

So why didn't I make the choices necessary to do that? Because nice girls just don't ask for help. They'd rather do almost anything than inconvenience other people. So they don't honor their own needs, desires, or dreams.

Underneath, they really don't think it's okay to do that.

Now and then I got involved in some form of ministry I really loved. From the time I was a little girl I was drawn to those living in poverty, and I went to college to become a social worker. When we started Willow Creek, my dream was for our church to become a community of people radically committed to compassion and justice. I served in our first ministry partnerships in the inner city of Chicago and went on some of our first serving trips to Latin America. I lived in an affluent suburb, but sitting in a squalid shanty town in Mexico passing out canned peaches to little barefoot kids was really where I felt most at home and most alive.

....

But whenever my involvement in ministry seemed to inconvenience Bill or the kids, or in any way kept me from living up to other people's expectations—which it always did—then I withdrew, backed out, quit. When I felt frustrated, or even angry, about having to do that, I confessed my sin, my selfishness, my demanding spirit.

I thought that was the right thing to do. I thought denying my gifts and passions was part of what it meant to "die to self," as Scripture requires. I didn't realize there was a difference between dying to self-will and dying to the self God created me to be.

Yes, we must live according to the ebb and flow of life's seasons, and our movement

between ministry within the home and beyond the home must shift according to the needs of those seasons. I think this is true for both men and women, both fathers and mothers.

And yes, there is a necessary sacrifice—a suffering even—that is part of the life of every servant of Jesus. We need to ask for grace and strength to endure these challenges.

But . . .

If year after year our lives are consumed with activities we've been neither gifted nor impassioned to do, and we never have a chance to slide into the sweet spot of giving out of our true self, we pay a higher price in ministry than God is asking us to pay. And the saddest thing is, when we allow this to happen, nobody wins.

I thought I was sacrificing parts of myself for the sake of others, but you know what?

Bill didn't win. He married me, in part, because he fell in love with the confidence, competence, and energy for life and ministry he saw in me. But decades of ignoring, neglecting, and denying my true gifts and passions had drained me of the very vitality he had been drawn to, and left me feeling incompetent and insecure—not at all the person Bill hoped to share his life with. So my husband didn't win.

Our kids didn't win. They got a very devoted, conscientious mother, who picked up after them, made sure they got their homework done, and took them wherever they needed to go without complaining. They got a mother who adored them, prayed for them, always wanted the best for them. But they didn't get a joyful mother. They didn't get a fun mother. They didn't get to see, up close and personal, a woman fully alive in God.

My son needed to see that in his mom, but even more, my daughter needed to see that. She needed to see me operate out of strength and passion, and I couldn't give her that. Fortunately, there were other women in her life who modeled that for her. And I am grateful that as I have chosen to lean into my own true life, I am now able to give her something I couldn't give her before. But if I had it to do over, I would not have waited so long. I would not have robbed her of the mentoring model of an authentically engaged mother.

....

My church did not win. It was clear our church needed Bill. He has been an extraordinary pastor. I never wanted to hinder what he could offer to our church, and I certainly don't want to now. But my church needed me too, not because I am anything special but simply because it is where God put me, and God put me there for a reason. God gave me a unique perspective and worthy dreams. God gave me words and influence to use for good. But I didn't use them. I didn't show up. I might have been there physically, but my gifts—my soul—didn't show up. I didn't value what I had to offer enough to actually offer it.

What about you? Are you showing up?

I hope you realize how much your family,

your friends, your church, your community, and this world need you. Don't allow who you truly are to be lost, buried, or devalued. What is in you matters. What is most truly you matters. You have learned lessons, experienced pain, known joys, and gained a perspective nobody else has. You have an answer to the world's needs that is yours alone.

Whether God has called you to set up shop in a big corner office or at your kitchen table; to minister to large groups or to one person in need; to give forty hours a week or to be responsive to unexpected moments here and there; what you have to offer matters.

I know what it's like to wear a life that's not my own. But I'm learning to shed that restrictive robe and just put on me. I've discovered that's where my power is and where my joy is. I suspect that's where yours is too.

A good woman
doesn't let fear stop her.

A third thing I have learned about a good woman is that she sings her song even if she's terrified. Whatever she's called to do, she does it, even if she's so scared her voice breaks, her hand shakes, and her stomach aches. She doesn't let fear stop her.

Some years ago, when I was in a really desperate place of not knowing what to do with myself, I went away alone for a few days to do one simple thing: pray for guidance.

I said to God, "I don't know how to move

into the future. So I am going to pray for your guidance. I am going to listen for your voice. And then I am going to do whatever you tell me to do."

This is what I sensed God saying to me in response. *Okay, I will guide you. I will lead you into the future. But if you really want my guidance, you better get ready for an adventure. You better prepare yourself for new challenges and unexpected opportunities. You better get ready to learn, and stretch, and grow.*

Honestly, that is not what I hoped to hear. I wasn't looking for adventure—just a nice enjoyable life. But I'd already told God I would do whatever he said, so I decided to accept the adventure, whatever it was.

A short time later, I received a telephone call.

It was an invitation to travel to Northern Ireland and speak several times at a church near Belfast. I immediately said, "No. Absolutely not!" I was sure this was not the adventure God had in mind for me.

Traveling to Northern Ireland to speak might sound like a dream to some women, but it was the last thing I wanted. At that point I had done enough public speaking to know it was definitely not on my list of favorites. In fact, speaking to groups produced so much fear and trauma for me, that every time I did it I vowed I would never do it again.

Also, I was definitely not a fan of interna-

tional travel. I can't sleep on planes or in hotel rooms. I don't like constant change, and I'm not too fond of the unknown either. A good traveler I am not.

Yet, when I said, "No, I am not going to Northern Ireland to speak," I sensed God saying, *Yes you are.*

"But I'm too afraid," I said.

If you weren't afraid would you want to do this?

I thought about the women at the church in Belfast. I thought about the trouble and pain in their lives. I thought about what a privilege it would be to stand before them as a fellow struggler and remind them that God loves them and wants to walk through life with them.

. . . .

And I thought, "Yes, if I weren't so afraid, I would want to do this."

Then go. Don't let fear stop you.

I realized I had allowed fear to stop me too many times in my life. It was almost like I had two selves, a true self and a fearful self. My true self wanted to shout yes! to the challenges of life. My true self wanted to give, and serve, and make a difference.

But my fearful self constantly said, "No. You can't do that. You might fail. You might embarrass yourself. You might disappoint people."

Then I came face to face with the realization that disappointing people is the greatest fear of the nice girl. It truly was my deepest fear. It was bad enough when I was growing up anonymously in Kalamazoo, Michigan. But when I became Lynne Hybels, pastor's wife, it just got worse.

The voices in my head were ruthless. I imagined all the cutting things people might say about me. "Oh, *you're* Bill Hybels' wife? You're *it?* I thought you'd be younger, older, taller, shorter, 'Dutcher,' prettier, blonde. I thought you'd be a great Bible teacher or a powerful leader. I thought you'd be more dynamic, more subdued, more outgoing, more demure, deeper, shallower, more fun, more profound. In general, I just thought you'd be more . . . impressive. I thought you'd be one of the 'superstars,' but you're just this ordinary person."

The many ways I could disappoint people

were all worked out in my mind. In all honesty, I actually did hear people say things like that sometimes—not a lot, but just enough to confirm the vicious dialogue running through my head. I couldn't face that. I couldn't open myself up to such colossal potential for disappointing. So I hid out. I didn't show up. I stayed in the background where it was safe.

And I missed out—on potential pain, yes, but also on the potential of being used by God.

For years, my true self, who wanted to say yes to God, had been pushed down and silenced by my fearful self. I knew it was time to end that pattern. I didn't want fear to hold me back anymore.

I said yes to the Northern Ireland trip.

. . . .

I wish I could tell you my fearful self just rolled over and died the moment I said yes. But it didn't.

On the contrary, it screamed more loudly than ever. "You made a terrible mistake. You will fail. Cancel the trip right now!"

I wanted to cancel the trip, but God said, *Ignore the fear. Trust me. Do what I've called you to do.*

I wrote the talks and I went to Northern Ireland. Of course, fear went too and told me that every talk I had written was terrible. Every afternoon before I spoke I had to say to fear: "Just be quiet. God has called me to do this and I'm going to trust God."

Every night I was in awe that God could use someone so weak and fearful. I returned home with the wonderful memory of a great adventure.

And I learned an important lesson. I learned that I didn't really know myself very well. I thought I did, but fear always hides the truth. Fear magnifies our weaknesses and it hides our potential. Only God knew the real me and the path I needed to be on. Only God could lead me into the future that was right for me.

I've also learned that my first response to just about everything is fear. If I listened to the voice of fear, I would do basically nothing. But part of what it means for me to move from being a nice girl to being a good woman, is that I choose to talk down fear. When fear says,

"What have you gotten yourself into now?" I say, "I think I've gotten myself into the will of God, and I'm not going to back down."

When fear says, "You are not smart enough, experienced enough, or strong enough to do what you're trying to do," I say, "Well, I serve a God who specializes in using people as flawed as me, so you might as well give up."

When fear says, "You are going to disappoint people so badly," I say, "Well, maybe so, but I guess I'd rather take the risk of disappointing people by not being good enough than disappoint God by not being brave enough."

When fear pulls out the stops, I borrow from God's words to Timothy: "Lynne, I have not given you this spirit of fear. I have given you a spirit of love, and of power, and of a sound mind."

And I claim the words of God to Joshua: "Lynne, have I not commanded you? Be strong and courageous. Do not be terrified; do not be discouraged, for I am the Lord your God and I will be with you wherever you go."

Do you have a fearful self that holds you back and tries to convince you that you could never be a world-changer? Maybe it's the fear of saying honestly to God, "I can't keep striving for your love. I'm tired, and I need to rest." I know how frightening it is when your whole relationship with God has been based on being busy for God.

Maybe it's the fear of saying to the people close to you, "Hey, I need to live my own life. I can't just keep picking up the pieces of yours." Again, I know how scary that is. Will they love you if you start honoring your own life? Will they still value you?

Or maybe it's the fear of failing if you do try to live your own life. Here's a confession: As unhappy as I was with the task-oriented, detail-intensive, administrative nightmare of my life, as long as I stayed buried in that, I never had to face the fear of throwing myself into something I really wanted to do—I mean really putting myself out there—and then failing.

As long as the life I really wanted was just theoretical, I could tell myself, "If I had the freedom I deserve, I could do this great thing for God. . ." But if I actually made the choices necessary to do it, I might discover that I couldn't do it. I might fail.

So I kept finding reasons not to try.

It took me almost thirty years in ministry to be willing to fail. I am not proud of that. And the truth is, what finally pushed me over the

ledge was turning fifty and realizing that life is short, and if I didn't start living it, I might never have the chance.

Some time ago, I watched my friend Holly run the Chicago Marathon. While I was standing on the sidelines looking for her, a woman ran by wearing a T-shirt that said on the front, "Done watching." On the back it said, "Doing."

I couldn't hold back the tears.

I cried for two reasons. One, because I don't want to just watch the race of life anymore. I want to run it. *Done watching. Doing.*

Two, I cried because that woman, and my friend Holly, were running in a pack of women who were all cheering one another on. Some were running strong. Some were doubled over with the pain. And some literally had to be carried across the finish line. But they did it together.

You know what some of us fear more than anything else? Each other. I feared other women's success because I thought it made me look bad. I feared other women's choices because I thought they invalidated my choices. I feared getting close to other women because

I was miserable and I didn't want them to know that.

So for years I lived in isolation. I lived outside community; I lived without a tribe. And I suffered for that. I needed women to listen to my pain and honor my tears. Then, I needed women to tell me it was time to dry my tears, get off my ... chair ... and do something. I needed women to grab my hands and say, "Let's pray about this." Then I needed women to tell me to rent a silly movie that would make me laugh hysterically. I needed women to say, "You have gifts, and you feel strongly about certain things, and we are not going to let you withdraw from life. You need to show up." Then I needed women to say, "Lighten up!

Celebrate! Go shopping and add a little color to your black wardrobe." I needed women to say, "Who you are is okay, and we love you for it." And I still need that.

The best thing I ever did was tiptoe out of isolation and join the circle of women. We need to choose to believe we are all in this together. We need to accept and honor our own lives so we can accept and honor each other's lives. When we do this, when we help one another, cheer one another on, call one another to our truest and highest selves, we become a powerful force for good—for God—in this world.

If ever the world needed an army of good women who dare to make a difference with their lives, it is now.

Margaret Mead said: "Never doubt that a small group of thoughtful, committed citizens can change the world." My version of that quote is: "Never doubt that a community of thoughtful, committed women, filled with the power and love of God, using gifts they have identified and developed, and pursuing passions planted in them by God—never doubt that these women can change the world."

a dangerous woman

At the beginning of this book I said that the opposite of a nice girl is a good woman. But what I really wanted to say—and what I'm going to say now—is that the opposite of a nice girl is not just a good woman, but a downright dangerous woman. A woman who shows up with everything she is and joins the battle against whatever opposes the redeeming work of God in our lives and in our world.

A dangerous woman delves deeply into the truth of who she is, grounds herself daily in the healing and empowering love of God, and radically engages with the needs of the world.

My move toward the realm of dangerous women was prompted by the realization that I was living without passion, energy, dreams. Inspiration came from dangerous women I met along the way. From college students and empty-nesters. Young moms and grandmothers. From women crossing lines of age, race and culture. Women mentoring one another and sharpening skills. Women volunteering time. Raising money. Thinking creatively. Taking risks. Reinventing their lives. Following their God-given dreams.

Dangerous women. World-changing women.

That's what I want to be and that's what I hope you will be. All of us. Together.

May we be dangerous women.

May we be women who acknowledge our power to change, and grow, and be radically alive for God.

May we be healers of wounds and righters of wrongs.

May we weep with those who weep and speak for those who cannot speak for themselves.

*May we cherish children, embrace the elderly,
and empower the poor.*

May we pray deeply and teach wisely.

May we be strong and gentle leaders.

May we sing songs of joy and talk down fear.

*May we never hesitate to let passion push us,
conviction compel us, and righteous anger
energize us.*

*May we strike fear into all that is unjust and evil
in the world.*

*May we dismantle abusive systems and silence
lies with truth.*

*May we shine like stars in a darkened
generation.*

May we overflow with goodness in the name of God and by the power of Jesus. And in that name, and by that power, may we change the world.

Dear God,
Please make us dangerous women.
Amen.

Some of the most amazingly dangerous women I have met live on the continent of Africa. Lacking everything from education to clean water, and battling the deadly force of HIV/AIDS, these women are working, praying, and courageously creating a better world for their children and for the millions of orphans in their care.

My first trip to Africa broke my heart. Subsequent trips pushed me to action.

A portion of the royalties from this book will be donated to Willow Creek Community Church ministry partners in South Africa and Zambia who provide food, education, medicines, and job opportunities for widows, orphans, and people infected with HIV/AIDS.

ABOUT THE AUTHOR

Lynne Hybels joined her husband, Bill, in starting Willow Creek Community Church in 1975. She has edited many books and is coauthor of *Rediscovering Church* and *Fit to Be Tied*. She has been involved in Willow Creek's ministry partnerships in Latin America and currently serves as an advocate for those affected by HIV/AIDS in Africa. Lynne and Bill live in a suburb of Chicago and have two adult children.

WILLOW

Willow Creek Association
P.O. Box 3188
Barrington, Illinois 60010-3188
www.willowcreek.com